RAND COUNTERINSURGENCY STUDY • PAPER 2

OCCASIONAL PAPER

Subversion and Insurgency

William Rosenau

Prepared for the Office of the Secretary of Defense

NATIONAL DEFENSE RESEARCH INSTITUTE

The research described in this report was prepared for the Office of the Secretary of Defense (OSD). The research was conducted in the RAND National Defense Research Institute, a federally funded research and development center sponsored by the OSD, the Joint Staff, the Unified Combatant Commands, the Department of the Navy, the Marine Corps, the defense agencies, and the defense Intelligence Community under Contract W74V8H-06-C-0002.

ISBN 978-0-8330-4123-4

Published 2007 by the RAND Corporation
1776 Main Street, P.O. Box 2138, Santa Monica, CA 90407-2138
1200 South Hayes Street, Arlington, VA 22202-5050
4570 Fifth Avenue, Suite 600, Pittsburgh, PA 15213-2665
RAND URL: http://www.rand.org/
To order RAND documents or to obtain additional information, contact
Distribution Services: Telephone: (310) 451-7002;
Fax: (310) 451-6915; Email: order@rand.org

Preface

If the U.S. armed forces, the intelligence community, and civilian agencies expect to wage effective counterinsurgencies in Iraq and Afghanistan, they need to develop more sophisticated approaches to counter subversion, which has become an important element of the insurgent repertoire. This paper presents a set of case studies to explore the elements of subversion in-depth. It discusses preliminary ideas for combating subversive activities in the context of the war against violent Islamic extremism and concludes with a discussion of how U.S. support for countersubversion within authoritarian regimes can conflict with other important U.S. foreign policy objectives, such as the promotion of human rights.

This research was sponsored by the Office of the Secretary of Defense (OSD) and conducted within the International Security and Defense Policy Center (ISDP) of the RAND National Defense Research Institute, a federally funded research and development center sponsored by OSD, the Joint Staff, the Unified Combatant Commands, the Department of the Navy, the Marine Corps, the defense agencies, and the defense Intelligence Community. This research is part of a larger RAND effort to develop a roadmap for long-term investment in Department of Defense counterinsurgency capabilities. For more information on the ISDP, please contact its director, James Dobbins. He can be reached by email at dobbins@rand.org; by phone at 310-393-0411, extension 5134; or by mail at the RAND Corporation, 1776 Main Street, Santa Monica, California 90407-2138. More information about RAND is available at www.rand.org.

Contents

Acknowledgments

The author would like to thank Alan Vick and David J. Kilcullen for their very thoughtful reviews of this paper. In addition, the author would like to acknowledge the members of the RAND Insurgency Board for their helpful critique of an earlier version of this paper. The author also wishes to thank Jim Dobbins and John Gordon for their support, and John Parachini and the Intelligence Policy Center for providing staff development funds to complete this paper.

Subversion and Insurgency

> Americans are politically naïve, and it is difficult to make them realize that they face opponents who do not play by the rules.
>
> *Guenter Lewy, 1987*

> To totalitarianism, an opponent is by definition subversive; democracy treats subversives as mere opponents for fear of betraying its principles.
>
> *Jean-François Revel, 1984*

Introduction

Persistent insurgencies in Afghanistan and Iraq, and the emergence of what some analysts, journalists, and politicians have described as the "global jihad" have helped renew interest in the question of how insurgents employ subversion. In Iraq, according to the U.S. Defense Intelligence Agency, the new government is threatened by "[s]ubversion and infiltration of emerging government institutions [and] security and intelligence services" (Jacoby, 2005, p. 8). More broadly, international "jihadis" are using violence and subversion to establish a "totalitarian empire that denies all political and religious freedom," according to the *National Security Strategy of the United States of America* (White House, 2006). John Mackinlay (2005, pp. 51–52) argues that the subversion of vulnerable Muslim populations is a critical component of the "complex insurgency" being waged by Osama bin Laden and others within the jihadi firmament.

But despite this renewed recognition that terrorists and insurgents employ subversion—and a general agreement with the late J. Bowyer Bell's (1994, p. 135) assertion that armed rebels of all varieties are "practiced subversives"—little systematic attention has been devoted to the topic in recent years. For decades, scholarly and policy-oriented research on the topic has been nonexistent. Perhaps the lack of analytical focus can be explained by the term's lingering Cold-War era connotations of rampant political paranoia, repression, and the relentless

An earlier version of this paper, "Subversion and Terrorism: Understanding and Countering the Threat," appeared in the Memorial Institute for the Prevention of Terrorism's *MIPT Terrorism Annual*, 2006.

hunt for internal enemies. Indeed, during the Cold War, American policymakers sometimes described the threat of communist subversion in overheated language that bordered on the comical, as U.S. Secretary of State Dean Rusk did in April 1962, when he declared that urgent action was required before the "enemy's subversive politico-military teams find fertile spawning grounds for their fish eggs" (quoted in William Rosenau, 2005, p. 88).

Whatever the reason for the current inattention, it would be useful to explore the subversive challenge in more depth. Subversion is an important element of the insurgent repertoire, and if the U.S. armed forces, the intelligence community, and civilian agencies expect to wage effective counterinsurgency in Iraq and Afghanistan, they will have to develop more sophisticated approaches to counter subversion. The problem is not limited to these two countries, of course. As the "global war on terrorism" evolves into the "long war," it seems obvious that the United States and its friends and allies will necessarily encounter other insurgent adversaries, and those adversaries will likely employ subversion.[1]

As a first step in developing a more complete understanding of subversion, and what is required to counter it, this paper will begin with a discussion of definitions of subversion. Next, it will use a set of case studies to explore in more depth the elements of subversion identified in the section on definitions. The paper will go on to present a set of preliminary ideas for combating subversive activities in the context of the emerging long war against violent Islamic extremism. The paper will conclude with a brief discussion of how U.S. support for countersubversion within authoritarian regimes can conflict with other important U.S. foreign policy objectives, such as the promotion of human rights. Indeed, widespread domestic and international criticism of U.S. internal security assistance to repressive but nominally pro-Western governments helped end most U.S. aid to foreign police forces by the mid-1970s.[2]

Several caveats are in order, however. First, this paper is intended to serve as a reintroduction to the subject of subversion. It is not intended to be comprehensive or definitive, and additional research is required. Second, while some definitions identify propaganda as a component of subversion, propaganda will not be considered explicitly, since terrorist and insurgent use of such techniques has already been covered extensively in relatively recent academic and professional military literature.[3]

While terrorism and insurgency share some significant features (e.g., both are forms of violence employed by nonstate actors to further political objectives) (Tucker and Lamb, 2006, p. 1), they are of course distinct phenomena. As many analysts have noted, terrorism is a tactic strategy, while insurgency is a political-military one.[4] However, the line between terrorism

---

1 For more on what the U.S. Department of Defense (DoD) is calling "irregular warfare," see DoD, 2006.

2 For more on this point, see U.S. Congress, 1976.

3 See for example Weimann, 2004; and Schleifer, 2003.

4 The term *terrorism,* as used in this paper, is taken from the U.S. Department of State (DoS) (2005) definition, which categorizes it as "premeditated, politically motivated violence perpetrated against noncombatant targets by subnational groups or clandestine agents." Insurgency is defined as "a protracted political-military activity directed toward completely or partially controlling the resources of a country through the use of irregular military forces and illegal political organizations." This definition was used by the U.S. Central Intelligence Agency during the 1980s, and it remains useful. (See Byman et al., 2001, p. 4).

and insurgency is easily blurred, since most insurgent groups also engage in terrorism to a greater or lesser degree. Armed political movements that clearly meet most definitions of insurgency, such as the Liberation Tigers of Tamil Eelam (LTTE), the Communist Party of the Philippines/New People's Army, and the *Fuerzas Armadas Revolucionarios de Colombia* (Revolutionary Armed Forces of Colombia), have been designated by the U.S. State Department as "foreign terrorist organizations." The term "terrorist" is both a normative and a political label, and "governments will often attempt to condemn their opponents as terrorists, since the public relations victory achieved by this linguistic sleight of hand can be crucial in any ensuing struggle for popular support," as Conor Gearty (1992, p. 15) has observed. "Insurgent," on the other hand, connotes at least some measure of legitimacy, which explains why incumbents typically refuse to describe their adversaries as such.[5] The three groups considered in the case studies—the LTTE, the National Liberation Front for the Liberation of Vietnam (NLF, better known as the Viet Cong), and the *Frente Farbundo Martí de Liberación Nacional* (Farbundo Martí National Liberation Front, or FMLN) in El Salvador—are organizations to which *both* terms have been applied.

Third, this paper does not consider the subversive activities of al Qaeda and other salafist-jihadi movements in the depth they deserve—a shortfall the author hopes to redress in subsequent research. The infiltration of mosques, schools, and other Islamic institutions, the use of the Internet, and the radicalization and recruitment process in Western Europe and elsewhere are novel forms of subversion that are clearly distinct from Cold-War era subversive phenomena and, as such, require further research. That said, the following analysis will touch on the subversive activities of Islamist preaching and proselytizing (*da'wa*) organizations such as Hizb-ut-Tahrir (HT), which spread extremist ideology through missionary activities (*Algemene Inlichtingen- en Veiligheidsdienst* [AIVD], 2004, p. 27). While ostensibly nonviolent—and thus, falling outside any strict definition of insurgency—HT, with its transnational operations, extremist ideology, and clandestine structure, serves as an important recruiting ground for violent Islamist extremist groups (Khamidov, 2003, p. 6).[6]

Finally, it should be mentioned that the cases below, although focused on non-Islamist groups, provide insights that are useful when developing strategies and tools for countering jihadi subversion. That subversion has novel features, as mentioned above. However, it is essential to avoid the pitfall of assuming that al Qaeda and other elements of the jihadi "nebula" are utterly unique phenomena the likes of which humanity has never before encountered. Among other things, such an assumption can lead national security planners to the conclusion that every counterinsurgency campaign must begin *de novo*. There are no timeless "principles" of countersubversion, to be sure, but there are elements of earlier subversive campaigns that might help inform policymakers as they think about countering subversion in the context of the "long war." The Viet Cong, the FMLN, and the LTTE represent the upper end of subversive capabilities. Understanding how such movements employed subversion—while recognizing

---

[5] For more on this point, see Kilcullen, 2005, pp. 604–606.

[6] Al Qaeda has also reportedly infiltrated *da'wa* groups such as *Jama'at al-Tabligh*. "There are grounds for concern that, in the Horn of Africa, some Tablighs harbour militant agendas and that extremist groups may infiltrate Tabligh as a cover for their movements and contacts" (International Crisis Group [ICG], 2005, p. 18).

that it will take different forms among today's violent Islamist extremists—will better prepare us for contemporary counterinsurgency challenges.

Defining Subversion

Subversion, like terrorism and insurgency, has no universally accepted definition (Spjut, 1979, p. 254). For scholars such as Charles Townshend (1993, p. 116), the term is so elastic as to be virtually devoid of meaning, and its use does little more than convey the "enlarged sense of the vulnerability of modern systems to all kinds of covert assaults." Indeed, during the Cold War, the British Security Service (MI5) defined subversion as a generalized intention to "overthrow or undermine parliamentary democracy by political, industrial or violent means" (UK Security Service, 2005). Among American officials, "subversion" was an equally imprecise term, most often used when describing real or more fanciful clandestine efforts (by communists, typically) to undermine the United States and its friends and allies.[7]

For Moscow, too, subversion was something only one's adversary employed, but in reality, of course, both superpowers used subversion throughout the Cold War.[8] In the case of the United States, examples include Central Intelligence Agency (CIA) support to the Congress for Cultural Freedom (CCF), an organization of some of the world's leading intellectuals and artists that promoted liberal democratic alternatives to Soviet totalitarianism[9]; a secret "Marshall Plan for the mind" that distributed millions of copies of Western books in the Soviet Union and throughout the Warsaw Pact countries (Matthews, 2003); and covert assistance to trade unionists, politicians, journalists, military officers, and others in Chile opposed to President Salvador Allende, who was overthrown in a 1973 coup d'état[10]. Soviet subversion was even more extensive, and included the destabilization of democratic governments in Central and Eastern Europe during the late 1940s, covert support for liberation movements opposed to pro-Western regimes (e.g., to the *Frente Sandinista de Liberación Nacional* in Nicaragua during the 1960s and 1970s), and secret financial aid to pro-Soviet political parties, such as the Congress Party in India (Andrew and Mitrokhin, 2005, particularly chapters 3, 17 and 18, passim).

Within American and British military institutions today, the term has different connotations. For DoD, subversive activities are those actions "designed to undermine the military, economic, psychological, or political strength or morale of a regime" that do not fall into the categories of "treason, sedition, sabotage, or espionage" (DoD, 2001). The British Army contributes a useful refinement by identifying subversion as those activities "short of the use of

---

[7] See for example U.S. Congress, 1963.

[8] Among U.S. national security officials, such denials were intended for public, diplomatic, and political consumption. Behind closed doors, policymakers explicitly acknowledged that the U.S. government used subversion. During the Truman administration, for example, the National Security Council defined covert action to embrace "subversion against hostile states, including assistance to underground resistance movements, guerrillas and refugee liberation groups, and support of indigenous anti-communist elements in threatened countries of the free world" (DoS, 1948).

[9] For an interesting if tendentious account of the CCF, see Saunders, 1999.

[10] See for example U.S. Congress, 1975.

force" that are intended to erode the strength of the state (British Army, 2001, p. A-3-2). Under this definition, subversion can have violent manifestations—e.g., fomenting riots—and is typically employed as part of a broader armed terrorist or insurgent campaign, but it is essentially not martial in nature. In effect, subversion might be seen as a form of "non-violent terrorism."[11] Frank Kitson (1971, p. 3), the British counterinsurgency practitioner and theorist, defined subversion with characteristic directness as "all illegal measures short of the use of armed force taken by one section of the people of a country to overthrow those governing the country at the time, or to force them to do things they do not want to do." Although Kitson and other authors claim that subversion is sometimes employed in the expectation that such nonviolent actions on their own will lead to a government's downfall (Kitson, 1971, p. 83; Thompson, 1967, p. 28), examples of regime change by subversion alone are difficult if not impossible to find. More typically, terrorists and insurgents employ a double-edged sword, with subversion forming one edge, and the "armed struggle" the other.

Subversion sometimes precedes armed conflict; this was certainly the case with Maoist insurgencies during the Cold War. Analysts recognized the importance of identifying and counteracting subversion during the early stages of an insurgency, since the failure to do so would give the movement a time advantage that would be difficult and costly for the incumbent power to overcome (Jones and Molnar, 1966, p. 61). As such "popular" insurgent organizations matured and their mass base expanded, subversive activities typically became more overt, with riots and other "physical" manifestations forming a larger part of the movement's seditious repertoire. The current insurgency in Iraq's Anbar province has followed a different pattern. Contrary to classic Maoist doctrine, there was no protracted period of subversion in Anbar before insurgents and criminals took up arms relatively soon after the downfall of the Saddam Hussein regime in 2003.

However, it is worth noting that while most insurgent movements use subversion, a far fewer number of terrorist groups employ it. A lack of manpower is part of the explanation; small terrorist entities simply lack the personnel to engage in such activities in any substantial way. During the 1980s, left-wing European terrorist groups such as "17 November," the *Rote Armee Fracktion* (Red Army Faction, or RAF), and Action Directe each had fewer than 50 full-time members, and the Islamist "groupuscules" that carried out the 2004 Madrid railway station bombing and the 2005 attacks on the London transport system were even smaller. Terrorists may also be more predisposed to violent (as opposed to nonviolent or "less than violent") political behavior. While the subject of terrorist motivation is beyond the scope of this paper,[12] it should be mentioned in passing that violence appears to occupy a much more prominent place in the terrorist *mentalité* than it does in the insurgent worldview. Analysts have detected among individuals who become terrorists a burning desire to "escape the words"[13] and accelerate history through violent action. As one member of the Weather Underground said, "[w]e are tired of tiptoeing up to society and asking for reform, we are ready to kick it in the balls"

---

[11] The phrase is from Selznick, 1952, p. 238.

[12] For more on individual and group motivations, see Reich, 1998; and Hudson, n.d.

[13] The phrase is from Leites, 1979, p. 32. In della Porta's (1988) study of Italian left-wing terrorism, she notes that "previous experience in violent political activities predisposes individuals to involvement in terrorist groups."

(quoted in della Porta, 1988, p. 34). Finally, blood-drenched attacks are more likely than subversion to draw the media's gaze and, with it, the all-important attention of a wider audience (both domestic and international).[14]

Forms of Subversion

In addition to fomenting riots, what other activities might be characterized as subversive? Subversive actions can be grouped into three interrelated categories: (1) establishing front groups and penetrating and manipulating existing political parties; (2) infiltrating the armed forces, the police, and other institutions of the state, as well as important nonstate organizations; and (3) generating civil unrest through demonstrations, strikes, and boycotts. These categories will be discussed in turn below and will be explored more fully in the case studies.

Front Groups

To gain public credibility, attract new supporters, generate revenue, and acquire other resources, terrorist and insurgent groups need to undertake political activities that are entirely separate, or appear to be entirely separate, from the overtly violent activities of those groups. Sometimes this is achieved by infiltrating political parties, labor unions, community groups, and charitable organizations. Working in and through existing organizations, which provide a façade of legitimacy that might otherwise be unobtainable, terrorists and insurgents can bolster political allies, attack government policies, and attract international support. For those situations in which infiltration is too difficult, terrorists and insurgents may establish their own front groups—that is, organizations that purport to be independent but are in fact created and controlled by others. Front groups, notes John Thompson (2003), "can draw the sting of disapproval away from the cause and re-direct it against the state or institution that the terrorists are attacking." During the Cold War, front groups were established by many insurgent and terrorist groups, including the FMLN, the Viet Cong, and *Sendero Luminoso* (Shining Path). Today, groups as diverse as al Qaeda, the Kurdistan People's Congress (formerly known as the *Partiya Karkaren Kurdistan*), *Lashkar-i-Taiyibah* in Jammu and Kashmir, and the LTTE operate through political, social, and charitable fronts (Gunaratna, 2004, p. 95; Foreign Broadcast Information Service [FBIS], 2002; "Workers' Party," n.d.). Sinn Fein, the so-called "political wing" of the Provisional Irish Republican Army and arguably the most famous terrorist front in modern times, continues to serve as the respectable public face of Irish republican terrorism.

Infiltration

Terrorists and insurgents who penetrate state institutions can derive at least five significant benefits. The first is information: Infiltrating organs of the state, particularly the security forces, can help generate invaluable information about the government's capabilities, intentions, and weaknesses. Such infiltration, therefore, might be considered a form of intelligence collection

---

[14] As McCormick (2003, p. 496) observes, "[i]n a political sense, at least, terrorists begin to disappear when they drop off the headlines."

against the state. Second, penetration can give terrorists and insurgents opportunities to plant false information, redirect the state's potentially lethal gaze, force the authorities to misallocate resources, and otherwise derail the state's campaign. This too is a type of intelligence operation; like counterintelligence (CI) carried out by government intelligence services, it (secretly) aims to disrupt the organization and operations of enemy forces. Third, successful infiltration may lead to opportunities to steal government funds, weapons, equipment, and other resources. Fourth, penetration allows insurgents and terrorists to "talent spot" potential recruits and identify candidates for blackmail or bribery. Finally, infiltration can contribute to the terrorist and insurgent strategy of weakening and delegitimizing the incumbent power.[15] Just as infiltrators can help derail the state's counterterrorist or counterinsurgency campaign, so too can they degrade the state's ability to provide key public services by misdirecting resources, stealing funds, and spreading false and divisive rumors among those in the government workforce.

Infiltration of government institutions has been a tactic of revolutionaries at least since the time of Lenin, who concluded more than a century ago that "unless the revolution assumes a mass character and affects the troops, there can be no question of a serious struggle. That we must work among the troops goes without saying" (Lenin, 1900).[16] But the tactic is by no means confined to Marxist-Leninist groups. Al Qaeda reportedly claims to have infiltrated key government agencies within the United Arab Emirates (Lathem, 2006), and in Bangladesh, the radical Jamaat-e-Islami party, which sponsors a network of 15,000 guerrillas, has filled the country's armed forces, security services, and civilian agencies with its sympathizers (Harrison, 2006, p. 15). In Iraq, as mentioned above, insurgents have reportedly infiltrated the armed forces, the police, and intelligence services (Inspectors General, 2005, p. 22; "Insurgents," 2005). Such penetrations can have deadly consequences. An insurgent mortar attack on an Iraqi National Guard base north of Baghdad in October 2004 killed four and wounded 80; according to a press account (Schmitt and Shanker, 2004, p. 1), the attack "came at the exact time guardsmen were mustering for a ceremony, which is seen by experts as an indication that those firing off the mortars held inside information."

Finally, it must be mentioned that insurgent infiltration is not limited to state institutions, as again demonstrated today in Iraq. In Anbar province, insurgents have systematically infiltrated universities, where they reportedly occupy top academic and administrative positions. Iraq's oil industry, the country's most important economic sector, is also thoroughly penetrated by the insurgents, who have gone so far as to establish affiliated front companies to rake off illicit earnings.

Civil Unrest

As with infiltration, fomenting riots, organizing strikes, and staging demonstrations can have a corrosive effect on the power, presence, and capabilities of the state. Such unrest is first and foremost an affront to governmental authority, and the failure to suppress it can have damaging political repercussions for the state by demonstrating that it is incapable of living up to its

---

[15] For more on delegitimization as a strategy, see Harmon, 2001.

[16] There is an obvious parallel here between Bolshevik subversion and the subversive activities of such *da'wa* organizations as HT.

fundamental responsibility to maintain public order.[17] At the same time, however, overreaction by the security forces can play into the hands of terrorists and insurgents by seeming to confirm the opposition's claims about the fundamentally repressive nature of the state. The death of a demonstrator at the hands of the Berlin police in 1967 helped radicalize a generation of German young people, who came to believe that the Federal Republic of Germany was the Nazi regime reborn—a key component in the ideology of subsequent terrorist groups, most notably the RAF.[18]

Civil unrest can prove useful in a variety of other political and operational ways. Large-scale discord can deplete the resources of the state by forcing the authorities to deploy additional police, pay overtime, and in some cases send troops into the streets. With the security forces otherwise occupied, insurgents and terrorists gain a respite from the incumbent's campaign against them (U.S. Marine Corps Intelligence Activity, n.d. [1999]). Additionally, the greater presence of the security forces in response to unrest—in the form of patrols, roadblocks, and searches—can help the cause of the terrorists and insurgents by seeming to confirm the opposition's inevitable charge that the state has "militarized" the conflict and is now "at war" with people.

Strikes can cause serious economic damage. As Carlos Marighella observed in his *Minimanual of the Urban Guerrilla* (1969), perhaps the most widely read revolutionary "how-to" manual of the 1960s,

> strikes . . . although they are of brief duration, cause severe damage to the enemy . . . [by] disrupting daily life, occurring endlessly, one after the other, in true guerrilla fashion.

Even less violent forms of unrest, such as worker absenteeism, passive resistance, boycotts, and deliberate attempts to cripple government agencies by "overloading the system" with false reports, can have powerfully disruptive effects, both economically and politically (Molnar, 1963, p. 102). According to one scholar associated with HT, "a regime could be brought down through acts of civil disobedience such as strikes, non-cooperation with the authorities, or demonstrations" (quoted in ICG, 2003, p. 7).

Case Studies in Subversion

Although virtually every insurgent group and some terrorists employ subversive tactics, three organizations in particular are worth particular attention, given the high degree of emphasis they have devoted to these covert and clandestine activities. These cases are not intended to be representative; instead, they illustrate the high end of subversive capabilities. One group is contemporary, the two others are from the Cold War era, and while none is Islamist, the

---

[17] Such actions are part of a strategy for "[d]iscrediting, disarming and demoralizing the establishment," according to Clutterbuck, 1973, p. 275.

[18] For more on this point, see Varon, 2004, p. 39; and Becker, 1977) pp. 42–43.

three cases can generate insights that might be useful in the context of the campaign against al Qaeda and other jihadi groups.

Viet Cong: The Proselytizing Program

The communist opposition in South Vietnam embraced a strategy that employed both violent and nonviolent methods in an interconnected way. What Douglas Pike (1966), p. 85) termed the NLF's "violence program" included terrorism, guerrilla warfare, and conventional military operations. The NLF's "political struggle" included a range of actions intended to build support among the Vietnamese people, mobilize the population, and weaken the ability of the Saigon government to prosecute the war. For the NLF, however, the political struggle was by no means secondary to the armed campaign; rather, these two elements were conceptualized as equal and complementary components of the overall campaign against the Saigon regime (CIA, 1966, p. 14).

Particularly significant in terms of subversion were the front associations of farmers, teachers, students, and other sectors of Vietnamese society that allowed the NLF to exert control over the population, weaken the family and other social institutions, and offer a new form of security and belonging, which would be provided by the revolutionary movement (U.S. Information Service, 1967, p. 21). Front groups further aided the political struggle by spreading antigovernment rumors and mounting demonstrations intended to disrupt tax collection, conscription, or Army of the Republic of Vietnam (ARVN) operations against the Viet Cong (U.S. Information Service, 1967, p. 20).

What the NLF termed the *binh van* or "proselytizing" program, aimed at suborning ARVN and civilian government personnel, was a key feature of communist subversion in South Vietnam. According to the U.S. Information Service (1967, pp. 256–258), from its beginning in 1961, the program worked to:

- Encourage unit and individual desertions from the ARVN.
- Create discord between ARVN forces and government personnel and their U.S. advisors.
- Lower the morale of troops and civil servants, and encourage them to perform their duties in lackadaisical fashion.
- Promote pro-NLF activities and sentiment within government agencies and the armed forces.
- Create "an antiwar movement among the U.S. troops to weaken their fighting spirit and make them fear a protracted war" (South Vietnam Liberation Armed Forces, n.d. [1971]).

What techniques and tactics did the *binh van* program employ? Proselytizers used a spectrum of appeals, ranging from the target's sense of nationalism to anti-U.S. sentiment to the supposed inevitability of the NLF's victory (Pike, 1966, p. 258). These appeals were conveyed through leaflets and radio broadcasts, but direct, person-to-person communication was more important. Pike (1966, p. 264) describes what he terms a "classic *binh van* struggle":

> [It] typically would involve a sharp-tongued old woman buttonholing a young and ignorant private in the market place of a small village, berating him because of the killing and destruction of the war . . . and in general making him feel alien, miserable, and unpatriotic.

Blackmail and other forms of coercion sometimes played a role; soldiers and civil servants would be entrapped in a crime and then induced to serve as an NLF agent (Pike, 1966, p. 260). Promises of leniency and monetary rewards were offered to encourage desertion or defection. ARVN defectors and captured troops, using pamphlets, letters, and loudspeakers, urged their former comrades among Saigon's "puppet troops" to join the revolution ("Quang Da," 1972, p. 4). Families of soldiers were also key targets for NLF proselytizers. In the words of one NLF document ("NLF Binh Van," n.d. [1968]), "the families of the enemy's soldiers had to be convinced of the Revolution's righteousness." To lower troop morale, family members were encouraged to write to their sons in the ARVN about death, disease, and destruction on the home front.

The overall effectiveness of *binh van* is difficult to judge. Although Pike (1966, pp. 267–268) concludes that the program failed to achieve its ultimate goal of degrading Saigon's ability to wage war against the Viet Cong, we do know that tens of thousands of NLF members and supporters penetrated police and paramilitary forces, the intelligence services, the civil service, and the ARVN (Prados, 2002, p. 139), and that these institutions were plagued by low morale, corruption, and incompetence. Whether these deficiencies were a function of NLF subversive actions or were simply by-products of more systematic problems within South Vietnam is hard to assess. But given the size of the *binh van* effort, and the competence and sheer fanaticism of NLF cadres, it seems safe to conclude that subversion had some corrosive effect on Saigon's war effort.

The FMLN: Activating the Masses

El Salvador's FMLN, an umbrella organization composed of Marxist-Leninist political parties and guerrilla armies, employed many of the same subversive tactics used by the Viet Cong.[19] As with the NLF, the FMLN throughout the 1980s employed a two-prong strategy against the U.S.-backed government designed to weaken the regime militarily and politically and, ultimately, force it to collapse. FMLN military operations were intended to demonstrate the feebleness of the El Salvador armed forces and thus the pointlessness of American security assistance (CIA, 1984, p. 17). Alongside the armed struggle was a sophisticated political campaign intended to activate the masses and garner international support for the FMLN and international condemnation of the El Salvador government. As in Vietnam, front groups of peasants, workers, teachers, and students were employed widely. These fronts, in the words of a 1987 State Department study (DoS, 1981, p. 5), functioned as manpower pools for the guerrillas and were used to "stage demonstrations, disseminate propaganda, and occupy public

[19] FMLN leaders in fact made a close study of Vietnamese struggles against the French, the Japanese, and the Americans (Manwaring and Prisk 1988, pp. 162–164).

buildings—churches, foreign embassies, and government offices—as well as to augment guerrilla units."

They did so as part of the FMLN's strategy to isolate the government domestically and internationally, and to gain political and financial support for the insurgency (CIA, 1986b, p. 7). The FMLN's use of subversion differed from the NLF's in several interesting respects. First, given the relatively more industrialized nature of the Salvadoran economy, infiltration of labor unions and the creation of labor fronts were far more important elements in FMLN strategy. Factions and disarray within democratic trade unions made them vulnerable to penetration by the FMLN and its supporters. During the mid-1980s, unions dominated by or sympathetic to the rebels engaged in frequent work stoppages and organized major demonstrations against government ministries and private-sector firms (CIA, 1986a, pp. 13–14). More than 100 work stoppages and strikes took place in 1985 alone according to a U.S. government estimate (CIA, 1986b, p. 3).

And while the NLF relied on international front groups to raise funds and build support abroad for the revolution, the FMLN's use of foreign support networks was more formalized and gave the insurgency considerable strategic depth. In the United States, the Committee in Solidarity with the People of El Salvador (CISPES) was reportedly founded at the urging of Farid Handal, brother of Jorge Shafik Handal, the general secretary of the Communist Party of El Salvador, an FMLN component organization, to agitate on behalf of the insurgency (Arnold, 1987, p. B7). The FMLN also recognized the importance of the international human rights movement and exploited the real vulnerability of the Salvadoran government to charges that it systematically murdered and otherwise abused its political opponents. Human rights organizations created or infiltrated by the FMLN functioned as a "bullfrog chorus" that repeated charges of governmental abuses leveled by FMLN-controlled student and labor groups (CIA, 1986b, p. 6). Human rights activists linked to the FMLN maintained extensive ties to sympathetic trade unionists, clergy, students, and politicians in North America, Western Europe, and Latin America, and they were successful in persuading Dutch, German, and Greek parliamentarians to publicly criticize the Salvadoran government's admittedly abysmal human rights record (CIA, 1986b, p. 6). Finally, the FMLN was innovative in its use of domestic and international humanitarian and other nongovernmental organizations (NGOs) to generate financial resources. Donations from Western NGOs to FMLN fronts were a major source of insurgent funds (CIA, 1989, p. 16). Money from legitimate aid projects focusing on food, construction, medical care, and agricultural development was skimmed by individuals deemed "politically reliable" by the FMLN and then transferred to the guerrillas. Donors of course were never told that a portion of their contributions were destined for the FMLN (U.S. Defense Intelligence Agency, 1990, section 6).

As in the case of the NLF, it is difficult to assess the overall effectiveness of the FMLN's subversion campaign. American intelligence reports from the time suggested that despite widespread infiltration of trade unions, FMLN control was hardly total, as demonstrated by the fact that the insurgents were never able to call a general strike (CIA, 1989, p. 11). The gradual improvement of the government's human rights performance during the late 1980s undermined the credibility of FMLN-controlled human rights groups (CIA, 1986b, p. 6). That said, other aspects of the FMLN's subversive campaign must be judged a success. Front groups operating outside of El Salvador appear to have helped generate considerable international support for the FMLN, and they helped reduce the international standing of the El Salvador government. In addition, front groups made a notable contribution to insurgent resources by attracting donations from abroad and diverting to the FMLN.

The LTTE: Subversion on Five Continents

The operational sophistication of the Tamil Tigers is remarkable. The LTTE's cadre of suicide bombers, the so-called "Black Tigers," have raised suicide terrorism to an art form, having murdered Sri Lankan President Ranasinghe Premadasa in May 1991 and the Indian former prime minister, Rajiv Gandhi, two years later. But as remarkable as the LTTE's military capabilities are, the depth and sophistication of the Tamil Tiger's subversive activities are even more impressive and are probably without parallel among contemporary insurgent and terrorist organizations.

LTTE subversion takes place across five continents and includes a staggering number of front groups, including the Tamil Rehabilitation Organization (Bell, 2005a), the World Tamil Association, the World Tamil Movement (WTM), and the Federation of Associations of Canadian Tamils (FACT) (DoS, 2003, p. 114). In South Africa, the LTTE has infiltrated legitimate Tamil diaspora groups, including the Natal Tamil Federation and the South African Tamil Federation. It has established a network of sympathetic Tamil organizations across the country (Gunaratna, 1999), and LTTE operatives have reportedly infiltrated South African military units and intelligence services (Gunaratna, 2001).

LTTE front groups serve three purposes: As tools for hounding critics of the LTTE through demonstrations, mobs, and harassing phone calls, emails, and letters; as transmission belts for spreading LTTE propaganda within Tamil diaspora communities and among wider non-Tamil audiences; and for fundraising. During the late 1990s, the LTTE raised an estimated $1.5 million a month in the United Kingdom, Canada, and Australia alone (Byman et al., 2001, p. 50). However, the LTTE has relied on other sources of funds beyond Tamil diasporas. As with the FMLN, the Tamil Tigers skim money donated to fronts and LTTE-dominated NGOs that provide social services and other support to Tamils in Sri Lanka and in the diaspora (Byman et al., 2001, p. 51). "It is part of the LTTE modus operandi to siphon off funds that are intended for rehabilitation programs in Sri Lanka," according to the Canadian Immigration and Refugee Board (quoted in Bell, 2005a).

Through CISPES, the FMLN sought to influence politics and policy within the United States by lobbying members of Congress, generating favorable press coverage, and mobilizing public support. In Canada, home to one of the world's largest overseas Tamil populations, the LTTE has mounted an even more sustained and sophisticated campaign to shape the political environment. Through its fronts, the Tamil Tigers have made a major effort to cultivate politicians, including members of parliament. Parliamentarians have attended pro-LTTE rallies staged by the WTM (Bell, 2005b, p. 57). In July 2000, Maria Minna, the minister for international cooperation, and finance minister Paul Martin (who later served as prime minister) attended a Tamil New Year's celebration in Toronto organized by FACT, a group designated as an LTTE front by the Canadian Security and Intelligence Service (CSIS) (MacCharles, 2001, p. A06).[20]

As with the other two cases examined in this paper, it is difficult to make a definitive judgment about the overall effectiveness of LTTE subversive activities. Although reportedly urged by CSIS to ban LTTE, Martin's Liberal government repeatedly refused to do so, but whether this was a function of Tamil Tiger subversion or a product of some other concern (e.g., civil liberties) is hard to say (Bell, 2006). However, as in the case of the FMLN, the LTTE clearly has employed front groups to attract and divert donations to the insurgency.

Preliminary Policy Recommendations

Subversion is perhaps most closely associated with Cold-War era, mass-based, Marxist-Leninist groups. While it is certainly true that communists from the time of Lenin onward have used subversion, a wide variety of other violent underground movements continue to employ these tactics. These range from ethno-nationalist terrorists—such as *Euzkadi Ta Askatasuna* (Basque Fatherland and Liberty), which has operated hundreds of political front groups in Spain's Basque region (Tremlett, 2003, p. 13)—to jihadis, who have used Muslim NGOs such as the International Islamic Relief Organization, Inc., to covertly fund terrorist activities (U.S. Congress, 2005, p. 17; "Islamic/Aegean," 2000). There are indications that elements within movements like the Muslim Brotherhood and HT, which serve as terrorist recruitment pools and as covert "transmission belts" for radical ideologies, are attempting to infiltrate the civil service, the judiciary, student groups, and such private companies as International Business Machines in Britain and elsewhere (AIVD, 2004, pp. 40–41; Zeyno Baran, 2005, p. 72; and Malik, 2005, p. 10). Infiltration of government ministries and the security forces, the use of front groups, and fomenting civil unrest are likely to remain key elements of the subversive repertoire of the terrorist and the insurgent. Indeed, even within the United States itself, terrorist infiltration of police forces poses a very real threat according to the deputy chief of the Los Angeles Police Department (Berkow, 2004).[21] In sum, subversion cannot be dismissed as a Cold War problem irrelevant to the "Global War on Terror" or the "long war."

Developing a more complete understanding of how terrorists and insurgents use subversion is an obvious first step in developing more effective responses. More research is needed, since the systematic study of subversion has long been neglected. For the reasons argued in this paper, subversion is likely to remain an important element of insurgency, but additional research is required to more fully understand subversion as it is evolving in the 21st century—for example, how do insurgents employ the Internet for subversive ends; what role may Islamic institutions such as mosques, schools, and cultural centers be playing in underground struggles; and how are prisons, as prime recruiting grounds, functioning as hothouses of subversion? State-sponsored subversion, as discussed above, was a feature of the Cold War, but as

[20] The government of Martin's successor, Stephen Harper, designated the LTTE as a terrorist group on April 10, 2006.

[21] In addition, violent, right-wing extremists have been infiltrating the U.S. armed forces according to the Southern Poverty Law Center (Holthouse, 2006; and Barry, 1999, quoted in Holthouse, 2006).

Iran's ongoing support for Shia violence in Iraq shows, it remains an instrument of statecraft. Exploring how and why states engage in subversion, and how it differs from state sponsorship in earlier periods, should be part of this research agenda. In short, it is essential for analysts and policymakers to reconsider subversion and to do so in a way that is not constrained by a Maoist or Cold War conceptual straightjacket, in which subversion is directed exclusively against the state.

In the meantime, policymakers should consider how three core countersubversive capabilities—CI, police capacity, and public information strategies—could be enhanced. Regardless of how insurgent use of subversion evolves over time, these tools are ones that any government facing a nascent or full-blown insurgency will want to have as part of its countersubversion repertoire. While considering these measures, U.S. government officials must be alert to the tensions that will inevitably arise between promoting effective countersubversion abroad and American values, particularly human rights.

Strengthen Counterintelligence

Al Qaeda operatives, according to published accounts, have penetrated the security services of several Middle Eastern countries (Bowers, 2005, p. 1). Iraq's armed forces appear to be heavily infiltrated, and given the prominent internal security role of the military in many developing countries, it seems likely that terrorists and insurgents will continue to view this institution as an enticing target for subversion. In Iraq and the wider Muslim world, and in those non-Muslim countries with significant Muslim populations, the penetration of key economic sectors, educational institutions, and charitable organizations is likely to remain an important insurgent objective.

Countersubversion is a branch of CI.[22] Unfortunately, the U.S. CI capacity developed during the Cold War has atrophied. Within agencies such as the CIA, the Federal Bureau of Investigation, and DoD, CI has long been viewed as a professional backwater. For many people, CI, like the term *subversion,* has unfortunate connotations—Cold-War style paranoia, the "wilderness of mirrors," and the relentless search for "the enemy within," both real and imagined. In recent years, CI has been starved of resources relative to other intelligence activities, and as a result, according to the Commission on the Intelligence Capabilities of the United States Regarding Weapons of Mass Destruction (the "Silberman-Robb" commission), U.S. CI remains "fractured, myopic, and only marginally effective" (The Commission, 2005, p. 486). In the words of one senior U.S. intelligence official, "counterintelligence is not a priority" (Gertz, 2006, p. 1).

CI includes a variety of missions beyond countersubversion, such as penetrating and disrupting hostile intelligence services. But CI provides an invaluable set of tools and tactics for identifying, monitoring, and neutralizing the subversive activities of terrorists and insurgents. The revival of the countersubversion component of CI should include the development of doctrine, which was virtually nonexistent even during the Cold War, with the exception of a few

[22] Countersubversion, according to DoD (2001), is "[t]hat aspect of counterintelligence designed to detect, destroy, neutralize, or prevent subversive activities through the identification, exploitation, penetration, manipulation, deception, and repression of individuals, groups, or organizations conducting or suspected of conducting subversive activities."

military manuals, which were typically little more than "laundry lists" of tasks and objectives with little explanatory power. New countersubversion doctrine could of course be used to train U.S. personnel, both military and civilian, but it could also serve as the foundation for country- or region-specific manuals for assisting internal security personnel abroad.

Build Police Capacity

Subversion is far more than just an intelligence problem. Well-trained, professional police, attuned to local conditions and capable of building and maintaining strong relationships with the public, can play an invaluable role. But if police are to be effective, they will also have to be trained to identify patterns—to "connect the dots," to use the post-9/11 cliché—so that subversive activity can be spotted and neutralized. Effective countersubversive policing creates a detailed picture of a community in a way that allows anomalies—the arrival of outsiders, the influx of large amounts of cash, or the change in leadership of a community group—to be detected. In this respect, countersubversive policing is a form of community policing that identifies emerging threats and works to neutralize them with the aid of local individuals and groups.[23] Countersubversive policing also entails criminal investigation, but as Dennis J. Duncanson (1971, p. 18) concludes, uncovering and neutralizing subversion goes well beyond routine detection:

> There is a far-reaching conspiratorial network available to cover the culprits' traces. Witnesses and informants are frightened to speak without elaborate precautions, while the detectives themselves may be exposed to the same perils as the people they are trying to free from fear.

Improving police intelligence capabilities will also be crucial. Traditional police intelligence focuses on building cases and, ultimately, making arrests. Effective countersubversion, on the other hand, requires police officers to think more like intelligence personnel by moving beyond a prosecutorial mentality and putting greater emphasis on understanding and disrupting subversive activities and organizations. In addition, good professional relationships between the police and intelligence services will also be crucial. Here, the British Special Branch (SB) model may prove relevant. In Britain, the SB, sometimes termed "political police," serves as a bridge between the MI5 and the conventional police. Among other things, SB officers can translate intelligence information and requirements into terms that make sense to the cop on the beat; at the same time, SB can put police information into a form that is useful to intelligence analysts.[24] SB played a leading role against anticolonial insurgencies in Africa, Asia, and the Middle East, and it could serve as a template for building countersubversive police capabilities against new adversaries.[25]

---

[23] For more on the police role in counterterrorism, see Howard, 2004.

[24] For more on SB, see Ensum, 2002.

[25] For more on the SB role in the Malayan "Emergency," see Sunderland, 1964.

Develop Public Information Strategies

Some aspects of countersubversion require covert or clandestine approaches, e.g., developing human sources within the organizations engaged in subversion. However, in many cases, exposing and publicizing subversive activities can do much to help neutralize them. As Kitson (1971, p. 199) reminds us, "[t]he once mysterious processes used by the organizers of subversion to turn a section of a people against its government have long ago been exposed for all to see," since many of its leading practitioners have written at length about their tradecraft.

The ability to remain invisible is arguably the most powerful weapon at the disposal of the terrorist and insurgent. This is particularly true during the early stages of the conflict, when the state has an enormous material superiority but typically is unable to "see" the opposition. Losing that invisibility, and being exposed to the gaze of authorities, can be lethal for an underground movement. Committing terrorist acts, and maintaining what Gordon McCormick (2003, p. 496) terms a "violent presence," is essential for attracting recruits and resources and for sustaining the group over time, but it brings with it the danger of exposure. Subversion is a form of deception. Donations are solicited on false pretexts, individuals are misled as to a front group's true purpose, and morale-shattering lies are spread within military units and government ministries. A public education campaign that exposes such deceit could do much to undercut the nonviolent elements of the insurgent or terrorist campaign.[26]

Civil Liberties and Countersubversion

Distinguishing subversion from legitimate expressions of political dissent is a problem only for democracies; for totalitarian regimes, all opposition is inherently subversive (Revel, 1984, p. 4). To build a thorough understanding of the subversive underground, CI operations will necessarily be directed against a wide range of antigovernment groups, some of which will be aversely affected by these intelligence forays (Spjut, 1978, p. 64). Countersubversion also entails more than simply identifying subversives and subversive activity—it may very well require repression (Spjut, 1978, p. 61). According to Robert Thompson (1967, p. 84), "[i]t is not the aim of the intelligence organization merely to penetrate the insurgent movement. Its aim, inside its own country, must be the total eradication of the threat." And in the judgment of David Galula (1964, p. 68), intelligence operatives should infiltrate subversive organizations "to disintegrate [them] from within."

For democratic states facing substantial subversive threats within its borders, (e.g., the Netherlands), the requirements of a vigorous countersubversion campaign will create painful dilemmas and undemocratic consequences, since countersubversion will almost certainly collide with the rights of free speech, free association, and related liberties. In the case of authoritarian regimes facing serious subversive threats (e.g., Egypt, Pakistan, and Saudi Arabia), their rulers are likely to dismiss human-rights objections to their operations on the ground that such actions are essential for national survival. But the United States should not dismiss such criticisms as mere expressions of a woolly-headed, flabby liberalism. Although the United States is

---

[26] A similar point is made in Hosmer and Tanham, 1986, p. 11.

eager to "build capacity" in the so-called "frontline" states, policymakers must also be alert to the fact that repression (in less-than-totalitarian states, at least) can help fuel rebellion (Crenshaw, 1995, p. 19).[27] Finally, U.S. officials must be alert to the possible reemergence of a chronic Cold War problem, namely, the negative political consequences created by American support for repressive regimes. In their foreign policies, as at home, democratic states must reconcile civil liberties and the requirements of countersubversion.

Conclusion

In the decade following the end of the Cold War, insurgency and counterinsurgency languished in obscurity, of concern to only a handful of military and civilian specialists. Insurgency and counterinsurgency never vanished from the world's strategic landscape, of course, but policymakers and analysts were preoccupied with other national security challenges, such as nuclear proliferation, ethnic conflict, and the rise of Chinese power. The outbreak of insurgencies in Afghanistan and Iraq and the wider post-9/11 campaign against violent Islamist extremism have aroused long-dormant interest in insurgency and counterinsurgency. Searching for answers on library shelves, military officers, policy analysts, and academic experts have dusted off the classic texts of David Galula, Frank Kitson, and Robert Thompson, and have reached even further back to reexamine T. E. Lawrence's *Seven Pillars of Wisdom*, Charles William Gwynn's *Imperial Policing*, and C. E. Callwell's *Small Wars*.

These texts continue to have much to offer today's practitioners, scholars, and analysts. This is as true in the case of subversion and countersubversion as it is with other aspects of insurgency and counterinsurgency discussed in the classic works. Kitson (1971, p. 78), for example, stresses the importance of psychological operations, since "wars of subversion and countersubversion are fought, in the last resort, in the minds of the people"—a conclusion as true today as when it was written in 1971. But while these texts remain useful, it is important to avoid the trap of seeing them as "skeleton keys" of insurgency and counterinsurgency, that is, as tools directly applicable at all times and in all places. Subversion is an enduring feature of insurgency, but like other aspects of the phenomenon, it has changed since the end of the Cold War. It will be the task of practitioners and analytical specialists to identify the nature and scope of those changes and what will be required to wage effective countersubversion in the future.

---

[27] Karagiannis and McCauley (2006, p. 321) note that "repression is most likely to encourage a social movement to adopt violent methods where the movement is excluded from institutional politics and suffers *indiscriminate* and *reactive* state repression" [emphasis in original].

Bibliography

AIVD—*see Algemene Inlichtingen- en Veiligheidsdienst.*

Algemene Inlichtingen- en Veiligheidsdienst [Central Intelligence and Security Service] (AIVD), *From Dawa to Jihad: The Various Threats from Radical Islam to the Democratic Legal Order,* The Hague: The Ministry of the Interior and Kingdom, December 2004.

Andrew, Christopher, and Vasili Mitrokhin, *The World Was Going Our Way: The KGB and the Battle for the Third World,* New York: Basic Books, 2005.

Arnold, Ron, "No 'Regular Ordinary Person,'" *San Diego Union,* July 6, 1987.

Baran, Zeyno, "Fighting the War of Ideas," *Foreign Affairs,* Vol. 84, No. 4, November/December 2005, p. 72.

Barry, Steven, "'Planning a Skinhead Infantry,'" 1999. Excerpts quoted in David Holthouse, *A Few Bad Men,* Montgomery, Ala.: Southern Poverty Law Center, July 7, 2006. Accessed July 13, 2006: http://www.splcenter.org/intel/news/item.jsp?aid=66

Becker, Jillian, *Hitler's Children: The Story of the Baader-Meinhof Terrorist Gang,* Philadelphia and New York: J. B. Lippincott Company, 1977.

Bell, J. Bowyer, "The Armed Struggle and Underground Intelligence: An Overview," *Studies in Conflict and Terrorism,* Vol. 17, 1994.

Bell, Stewart, "RCMP Calls Tamil Fundraising Group for Tsunami Victims 'Front for Tamil Tigers,'" *National Post* (Toronto), January 19, 2005a. Open Source Center (formerly FBIS).

———, *Cold Terror: How Canada Nurtures and Exports Terrorism Around the World,* Mississauga, Ontario: John Wiley & Sons Canada, Ltd., 2005b, p. 57.

———, "Tories Would List Tigers as Terrorists," *National Post* (online version), January 18, 2006. Accessed February 6, 2006: http://www.canada.com/nationalpost/news/story.html?id=1f4d7889-519a-42ef-a081-b655df64347e

Berkow, Michael, "Homeland Security: The Internal Terrorists," *Police Chief,* Vol. 71, No. 6, June 2004. Accessed March 9, 2006: http://policechiefmagazine.org/magazine/index.cfm?fuseaction=display_arch&article_id=319&issue_id=62004

Bowers, Faye, "US Unready for Rising Threat of Moles," *Christian Science Monitor,* April 8, 2005.

British Army, *Army Field Manual,* Vol. 1, "Combined Arms Operations," Part 10, "Counterinsurgency Operations" (Strategic and Operational Guidelines), Issue 1.0, July 2001.

Byman, Daniel, Peter Chalk, Bruce Hoffman, William Rosenau, and David Brannan, *Trends in Outside Support for Insurgent Movements,* Santa Monica, Calif.: RAND Corporation, MR-1405-OTI, 2001.

CIA—*see U.S. Central Intelligence Agency.*

Clutterbuck, Richard, *Protest and the Urban Guerrilla,* New York: Abelard-Schuman, 1973.

Commission on the Intelligence Capabilities of the United States Regarding Weapons of Mass Destruction, *Report to the President of the United States,* Washington, D.C.: The Commission, March 31, 2005.

Crenshaw, Martha, "Thoughts on Relating Terrorism to Historical Contexts," in Martha Crenshaw, ed., *Terrorism in Context,* University Park, Penn.: Pennsylvania State University Press, 1995.

della Porta, Donatella, "Recruitment Processes in Clandestine Political Organizations: Italian Left-Wing Terrorism," in B. Klandermans, ed., *International Social Movement Research,* Vol. I Greenwich, Conn.: JAI Press Inc., 1988.

DoD—*see U.S. Department of Defense.*

DoS—*see U.S. Department of State.*

Duncanson, Dennis J., "The Police Function and Its Problems," in Dennis J. Duncanson, Richard A. Yudkin, and Barry Zorthian, *Lessons of Vietnam: Three Interpretive Essays,* New York: Asian-American Educational Exchange, Inc., 1971.

Ensum, Joanna, "Domestic Security in the United Kingdom: An Overview," in *Protecting America's Freedom in the Information Age, Part III: Selected Background Research,* New York: Markle Foundation, October 2002, pp. 101–112. Accessed October 10, 2006:
http://www.markle.org/markle_programs/policy_for_a_networked_society/national_security/projects/taskforce_national_security.php

FBIS—*see Foreign Broadcast Information Service.*

Foreign Broadcast Information Service [FBIS], "FBIS Report: Pakistan: NGO Linked to UBL, Kashmiri Militants Appeal for Funds," SAP20021211000125, December 11, 2002.

Galula, David, *Counterinsurgency Warfare: Theory and Practice,* New York; Frederick A. Praeger, Publisher, 1964.

Gearty, Conor, *Terror,* London: Faber & Faber, 1992.

Gertz, Bill, "Counterintelligence Posts Vacant," *Washington Times,* February 10, 2006.

Gunaratna, Rohan, "LTTE Chase the Propaganda War in the ANC's South Africa," *Jane's Intelligence Review* (online edition), April 1999.

———, "Intelligence Failures Exposed by Tamil Tiger Airport Attack," *Jane's Intelligence Review* (online edition), September 2001.

———, "The Post-Madrid Face of Al Qaeda," *Washington Quarterly,* Vol. 27, No. 3 Summer 2004, p. 95.

Harmon, Christopher C., "Five Strategies of Terrorism," *Small Wars and Insurgencies,* Vol. 12, No. 3, Autumn 2001.

Harrison, Selig S., "A New Hub for Terrorism?" *Washington Post,* August 2, 2006.

Holthouse, David, *A Few Bad Men,* Montgomery, Ala.: Southern Poverty Law Center, July 7, 2006. Accessed July 13, 2006:
http://www.splcenter.org/intel/news/item.jsp?aid=66

Hosmer, Stephen T., and George K. Tanham, *Countering Covert Aggression,* Santa Monica, Calif.: RAND Corporation, N-2412-USDP, 1986.

Howard, Paul, *Hard-Won Lessons: How Police Fight Terrorism in the United Kingdom,* New York: Manhattan Institute, December 2004.

Hudson, Rex A., *Who Becomes a Terrorist and Why: The 1999 Government Report on Profiling Terrorists,* Guilford, Conn.: The Lyons Press, n.d.

ICG—*see International Crisis Group.*

Inspectors General, *Interagency Assessment of Iraq Police Training,* Washington, D.C.: U.S. Department of State and U.S. Department of Defense, July 2005.

"Insurgents 'Inside Iraqi Police,'" *BBC News,* September 21 2005. Accessed February 1, 2006: http://news.bbc.co.uk/2/hi/middle_east/4266304.stm

International Crisis Group (ICG), *Radical Islam in Central Asia: Responding to Hizb ut-Tahrir,* Asia Report No. 58, June 30, 2003.

———, *Somalia's Islamists,* Africa Report No. 100, December 12, 2005.

"Islamic/Aegean Terrorism Review 9 Aug," Open Source Center (formerly FBIS), August 9, 2000.

Jacoby, Vice Admiral Lowell E., "Current and Projected National Security Threats to the United States," statement for the record, Senate Armed Services Committee, March 17, 2005.

Jones, Adrian H., and Andrew R. Molnar, *Combating Subversively Manipulated Civil Disturbances,* Washington, D.C.: American University, Center for Research in Social Systems, October 1966.

Karagiannis, Emmanuel, and Clark McCauley, "Hizb ut-Tahrir al-Islami: Evaluating the Threat Posed by a Radical Islamic Group That Remains Nonviolent," *Terrorism and Political Violence,* Vol. 18, 2006.

Kilcullen, David J., "Countering Global Insurgency," *Journal of Strategic Studies,* Vol. 28, No. 4, August 2005, pp. 604–606.

Kitson, Frank, *Low Intensity Operations: Subversion, Insurgency, Peace-Keeping,* London: Faber and Faber, 1971.

Khamidov, Alisher "Countering the Call: The US, Hizb-ut-Tahrir, and Religious Extremism in Central Asia," Washington, D.C.: Saban Center for Middle East Policy, Brookings Institution, Analysis Paper No. 4, July 2003.

Lathem, Niles, "Qaeda Claim: We 'Infiltrated' UAE Government," *New York Post,* February 25 2006.

Leites, Nathan, "Understanding the Next Act," *Terrorism: An International Journal,* Vol. 3, No. 1–2, 1979.

Lenin, V. I., "Lessons of the Moscow Uprising," *Proletary,* No. 2, August 29, 1900, (rev. in *Lenin Collected Works,* Vol. 11, Moscow, 1965). Accessed December 13, 2005: http://www.marxists.org/archive/lenin/works/1906/aug/29.htm

Lewy, Guenter, "Does America Need a Verfassungsschutzbericht?" *Orbis,* fall 1987.

MacCharles, Tonda, "Alliance Questions Why Assets Not Frozen," *Toronto Star,* November 10, 2001.

Mackinlay, John, *Defeating Complex Insurgency: Beyond Iraq and Afghanistan,* Whitehall Paper 64, London: Royal United Services Institute, 2005.

Malik, Shiv, "How Militant Islamists Are Infiltrating Top Companies," *Independent on Sunday* (London), September 11, 2005, p. 10.

Manwaring, Max G., and Court Prisk, eds., *El Salvador at War: An Oral History,* Washington, D.C.: National Defense University Press, 1988.

Marighella, Carlos, *Minimanual of the Urban Guerrilla,* 1969. Accessed September 28, 2005: http://web.archive.org/web/20010421163235/www.geocities.com/CapitolHill/1587/miniman.htm

Matthews, John P. C., "The West's Secret Marshall Plan for the Mind," *International Journal of Intelligence and Counterintelligence,* Vol. 16, No. 3, 2003, pp. 409–427.

McCormick, Gordon H., "Terrorist Decision Making," *Annual Review of Political Science,* Vol. 6, 2003.

Molnar, Andrew R., *Undergrounds in Insurgent, Revolutionary, and Resistance Warfare,* Washington, D.C.: Special Operations Research Office, November 1963.

"NLF Binh Van Program—Circa 1968," Record 14887, Douglas Pike Collection, Unit 05—NLF, n.d. [1968]. See *The Vietnam Archive,* Texas Tech University, Lubbock, Tex. Accessed January 10, 2005: http://star.vietnam.ttu.edu

Pike, Douglas, *Viet Cong: The Organization and Techniques of the National Liberation Front of South Vietnam,* Cambridge, Mass., and London: MIT Press, 1966.

Prados, John, "Impatience, Illusion, and Asymmetry: Intelligence in Vietnam," in Marc Jason Gilbert, ed., *Why the North Won the Vietnam War,* New York: Palgrave, 2002.

"Quang Da PRP Zonal C.C. Directive on Binh Van Activities," record no. 151475, Douglas Pike Collection: Unit 05—National Liberation Front, June 20, 1972. See *The Vietnam Archive,* Texas Tech University, Lubbock, Tex. Accessed January 10, 2005: http://star.vietnam.ttu.edu

Reich, Walter, ed., *Origins of Terrorism: Psychologies, Ideologies, Theologies, States of Mind,* Washington, D.C.: Woodrow Wilson Center Press, 1998.

Revel, Jean-François, "Can the Democracies Survive?" *Commentary,* June 1984.

Rosenau, William, *US Internal Security Assistance to South Vietnam: Insurgency, Subversion, and Public Order,* London and New York: Routledge, 2005.

———, "Subversion and Terrorism: Understanding and Countering the Threat," in Memorial Institute for the Prevention of Terrorism, *MIPT Terrorism Annual,* Oklahoma City, Okla., 2006. As of December 8, 2006 http://www.mipt.org/Publications.asp

Saunders, Frances Stonor, *The Cultural Cold War: The CIA and the World of Arts and Letters,* New York: The New Press, 1999.

Schleifer, Ron, "Reconstructing Iraq: Winning the Propaganda War in Iraq," *Middle East Quarterly,* Vol. XIII, No. 3, Summer 2003.

Schmitt, Eric, and Thom Shanker, "Estimates by US See More Rebels with More Funds," *New York Times,* October 22, 2004.

Selznick, Philip, *The Organizational Weapon: A Study of Bolshevik Strategy and Tactics,* New York: McGraw-Hill Book Company, Inc., 1952.

South Vietnam Liberation Armed Forces, "Binh Van Work in 1971," Record 150003, Douglas Pike Collection: Unit 05—National Liberation Front, n.d. [1971]. See *The Vietnam Archive,* Texas Tech University, Lubbock, Tex. Accessed January 10, 2005: http://star.vietnam.ttu.edu

Spjut, R. J., "A Review of Counter-Insurgency Theorists," *Political Quarterly,* Vol. 49, No. 1, January 1978.

———, "Defining Subversion," *British Journal of Law and Society,* Vol. 6, No. 2, Winter 1979.

Sunderland, Riley, *Antiguerrilla Intelligence in Malaya, 1948–1960,* Santa Monica, Calif.: RAND Corporation, 1964. As of December 8, 2006 (Web only):
http://www.rand.org/pubs/research_memoranda/RM4172/index.html

The Commission—*see Commission on the Intelligence Capabilities of the United States Regarding Weapons of Mass Destruction.*

Thompson, John, *Other People's Wars: A Review of Overseas Terrorism in Canada,* Toronto, Ontario, Canada: Mackenzie Institute, 2003. Accessed January 11, 2005:
http://mackenzieinstitute.com/2003/other_peoples_wars4.htm#organizations.

Thompson, Robert, *Defeating Communist Insurgency: Experiences from Malaya and Vietnam,* London: Chatto & Windus, 1967.

Townshend, Charles, *Making the Peace: Public Order and Public Security in Modern Britain,* Oxford: Oxford University Press, 1993.

Tremlett, Giles, "Court Bans Eta Front Groups," *Guardian* (London), May 5, 2003, p. 13.

Tucker, David, and Christopher J. Lamb, "Restructuring Special Operations Forces for Emerging Threats," *Strategic Forum,* No. 219, Washington, D.C.: Institute for National Strategic Studies, National Defense University, January 2006.

UK Security Service, *About MI5,* London: UK Security Service, 2005. Accessed March 28, 2005: https://www.mi5.gov.uk/output/Page126.html

U.S. Central Intelligence Agency (CIA), Directorate of Intelligence, "The Vulnerability of Non-Communist Groups in South Vietnam to Political Subversion," record 31052, CIA Collection, May 27, 1966. See *The Vietnam Archive,* Texas Tech University, Lubbock, Tex. Accessed January 10, 2005: http://star.vietnam.ttu.edu

———, "El Salvador: Guerrilla Capabilities and Prospects over the Next Two Years: An Intelligence Assessment," MORI DocID: 761619, Washington, D.C.: National Security Archive, George Washington University, October 1984, p. 17.

———, "El Salvador: A Net Assessment of the War: An Intelligence Assessment," MORI DocID:761620, Washington, D.C.: National Security Archive, George Washington University, February 1986a.

———, "El Salvador's Insurgents: Resurrecting an Urban Political Strategy," MORI DocID:761621, Washington, D.C.: National Security Archive, George Washington University, September 1986b.

———, "El Salvador: Government and Insurgent Prospects," Washington, D.C.: National Security Archive, George Washington University, February 1989.

U.S. Congress, House, Committee on Foreign Affairs, *Castro-Communist Subversion in the Western Hemisphere: Hearings Before the Subcommittee on Inter-American Affairs,* 88th Cong., 1st sess., March 4, 1963.

———, Senate, Staff Report of the Select Committee to Study Governmental Operations with Respect to Intelligence Activities, *Covert Action in Chile 1963–1973,* 94th Cong., 1st sess., December 18, 1975. Accessed February 2, 2006: http://foia.state.gov/Reports/ChurchReport.asp

———, General Accounting Office, *Stopping US Assistance to Foreign Police and Prisons,* ID-76-5, Washington, D.C.: General Accounting Office, February 1976.

———, Government Accountability Office, *Information on U.S. Agencies' Efforts to Address Islamic Extremism,* GAO-05-852, Washington, D.C.: General Accounting Office, September 2005, p. 17.

U.S. Defense Intelligence Agency, "JTIC Special Advisory 05-90—Salvadoran Insurgent Repopulation of Their Strategic Rear Guard Areas, Part I," Washington, D.C.: National Security Archive, George Washington University, November 1990, section 6.

U.S. Department of Defense (DoD), *Dictionary of Military and Associated Terms,* JP 1-02, April 12, 2001 (as amended through August 31, 2005). Accessed February 1 and October 15, 2006:
http://www.dtic.mil/doctrine/jel/doddict/data/s/
http://www.dtic.mil/doctrine/jel/doddict/data/c/

———, *Quadrennial Defense Review Report,* Washington, D.C.: DoD, February 6, 2006.

U.S. Department of State (DoS), *Foreign Relations of the United States, 1945–1950: Emergence of the Intelligence Establishment,* Washington, D.C.: National Security Council, Directive on Office of Special Projects, NSC 10/2, document no. 292, June 18, 1948. Accessed July 20, 2006:
http://www.state.gov/www/about_state/history/intel/290_300.html

———, Bureau of Intelligence and Research, "The Insurgency in El Salvador," Washington, D.C.: National Security Archive, George Washington University, May 8, 1981.

———, Office of the Coordinator for Counterterrorism, *Patterns of Global Terrorism 2002,* Washington, D.C.: DoS, April 2003.

———, Office of the Coordinator for Counterterrorism, *Country Reports on Terrorism 2004,* Washington, D.C.: DoS, April 2005.

U.S. Information Service, Office of Policy and Research, "The Viet Cong: The United Front Technique," R-13-67, Record 128321, Douglas Pike Collection: Unit 06—Democratic Republic of Vietnam, April 20, 1967, p. 21. See *The Vietnam Archive,* Texas Tech University, Lubbock, Tex. Accessed January 10, 2005: http://star.vietnam.ttu.edu

U.S. Marine Corps Intelligence Activity, *The Urban Threat: Guerrilla and Terrorist Organizations,* n.d. [1999]. Accessed July 5, 2006: http://www.smallwarsjournal.com/documents/urbanthreat.pdf

Varon, Jeremy, *Bringing the War Home: The Weather Underground, the Red Army Faction, and Revolutionary Violence in the Sixties and Seventies,* Berkeley, Los Angeles, and London: University of California Press, 2004.

Weimann, Gabriel, *How Modern Terrorism Uses the Internet,* Washington, D.C.: United States Institute of Peace, Special Report No. 116, March 2004.

White House, *National Security Strategy of the United States of America,* Washington, D.C.: White House, March 2006. Accessed July 26, 2006: http://www.whitehouse.gov/nsc/nss/2006/sectionIII.html

"Workers' Party of Kurdistan (PKK)," Jane's Terrorism and Insurgency Centre, n.d. Accessed April 19, 2005: www4.janes.com